NEVER A STRAIGHT LINE
BERNICE LEVER

Library and Archives Canada Cataloguing in Publication

Lever, Bernice, 1936-
    Never a straight line / Bernice Lever.

Poems.
ISBN 978-0-88753-438-6

    I. Title.

PS8573.E953N48 2007   C811'.54   C2007-904121-3

The Palm Poets Series is published by Black Moss Press at 2450 Byng Road, Windsor, Ontario N8W 3E8.

Black Moss would like to acknowledge the generous support of the Canada Council and the Ontario Arts Council for its publishing program.

Le Conseil des Arts | The Canada Council
du Canada | for the Arts

ONTARIO ARTS COUNCIL
CONSEIL DES ARTS DE L'ONTARIO

LET'S GO HOME NOW

Evening's soft musk
brushes bright sunlight to sleep
flowers part for happy child
content with two balloons
to follow grandparent on cane
from this gentle parkette
sky complete with one white bird.

RELATIONSHIPS

Sweet or Very Otherwise

LEAVING

Burying first my grey hair
and tarnished silverware
I will garage-sale my slimy green fears
and red high heels.

Kayaking to the river's end
sloshing in noisy white foam
threading between boulders
and dark mud shores

Paddling unevenly
slicing sky and horizon
then circling upstream
for some weekends
all I need is syrupy moonshine
and my waterproof heart.

CARAPACE

We are sea turtles
clambering over slippery, sea-weeded rocks
searching for hidden morsels
lumbering sideways, to avoid much contact
our mouths always smiling
but our eyes, dark rounds, ever watchful.

Once we were soft shelled
easy to penetrate, and trying anything
even eager to share our space
creatively curling into combinations.

Now as aging turtles
we paddle alone, slowly
around tropical shorelines
eyeing possible mating or meal material
recalling our decades of encounters.

As each rasp against a jagged stone
caused scar tissues
those cuts from a colourful reef
built up wound on wound
even nips from hungry sharks
from our too slow tucking in limbs
all added to our crusty defences
as we built our fortress homes
bigger barriers or cunning challenges
to possible co-inhabitants.

Even turtles avoid known
        predators.

TOUCH

Somehow you live on your surfaces
    textures are all
sensation is everywhere heightened
    a fine cross hair
colours sharpen
    a kaleidoscope tunnel, then blur
blending one into each other
footfalls and waterfalls
echo your heartbeats
as you breathe
in one another.

10

SHAPING

Your hands, like the sea
that laps at its beaches
each promontory and fiord
are intimate with my every curve
smoothing my slack
molding into hardness
my every desire
with your caresses.

My body, worn as a rocky shoreline
or strewn with storm's wreckage,
is refreshed by your loving waters
cleansing me of pain
eroding terror
until your tears
join us in rainbow.

COVERING

There's an intimacy in a lover's bed
hugging the warmth
of the same eiderdown
smelling a lover's scent
on last night's pillows
soothing silken underwear
discarded on bedposts
empty with longing
for their owner
as you are.

12

HERE'S TO US

Perhaps, a toast with white wine
as floral shapes float
through crystal goblets

golden/cream/tangerine cosmos
in a windy rain
not wet lenses smeared
tiny tears on eye glasses
until the dark centres
become insect heads
flitting by now are
Monarch butterflies.

Wings and petals can be crushed
dried and discarded
but our moist vision goes on
as this painting bursts
our imagination's borders
as colours float softly
off this water colour
we renew our bonds.

A SECOND DISTANCE

Sometimes the distance is just a far-away place
where the twilight meets the lavender horizon
below some beckoning stars
to the sounds of swooping night birds,

sometimes the distance
is an unreachable lunar landscape
where all our dreams fly
free at last of all our inner storms,

14

sometimes the distance
is just the light disappearing
into the stillness behind your eyes
as a missing sparkle lost in tears,

sometimes the distance separates as lovers
as silence grows in secret places
so a darkness gathers clouding
the birth of each caring smile,

sometimes the distance
of this cool isolation space
warms up in the heat of your arms
and disappears as our eager lips meet.

LAWSON BAY ROAD

Not your traditional powdery brown road
leading through the expected autumn colours:
rusts, reds and earthy dry crisps

but vibrant explosions – yellows and oranges
pretending this is life
not the end of a season,

leaf colours so strong
they seem posters declaring
    This is My dream.

Fall may seem a mellow, warm acceptance
of winter: that white, blank death
but I dream only bright life
as my lake road leads to love.

FERRY ME

ferry me across
keep me floating
why ever reach the stony shores
sandbars of anchor is all we need

keep me rising, bobbing, cresting
never ebbing, always riding you

aflame

16

SIGNATURE MOVES

She in black stockings
snug fitting, tan sweater dress
reads her paperback silently
and slides her left foot softly
        slowly in and out
of her dark leather clog
stroking one ebony knee
and thigh against its mate

sending shivers up
to moist mouths – hers
and others, furtively watching
from plastic patio chairs
in this cool fall air,
this small area warmed
by this simple female friction
responding to her book's plot or pacing
as she nods black bangs
at each carefully turned page
unaware of what riotous
emotions she is unleashing.

YOUR NEMESIS

Unexpectedly, on a crowded elevator
or on a forlorn plateau
certain timbers or tones
drum beats or bird songs
unleash primeval urges.

Just as specific scents
soar passion's flight
whether jasmine or English leather
wild heather or Parisian expensive
you have a sudden flush of desiring
for what you had when your lover
exuded in that heated moment
exactly that same aroma.

Your senses   so interwoven into the fabric
of your past love matings
your hormones so fooled
by memory's forcefulness
emotions so beguiled by longing
that strawberry Margaritas
have you kissing the nearest lips.

LUSCIOUS

Ah, seductive suck
of dark, liquid pools
these mysterious black eyes
that mirror your desires
never letting you know
they have their own selfish whims
or whimsy to attain
that you are just their plaything
some toy, some Charlie McCarthy
mouthpiece, for their amusement
perhaps even gain
if you have anything to give.

Once your shell is dry
floating black lust will dive
into its next victim
who will praise its beauty
happily believing:
        here is fulfillment.

SCARCE AS ANGELS

Don't arrive printed
with a big capital 'O' stamped
clearly on their foreheads
    with simultaneous translation
    as the question to pursue

We've progressed
beyond 'A' for adultery
    Hawthorne deciphered that Puritan burr
that negative label that silenced
    the next 25 symbols
poor old 'O' more than half way down
    the winning stretch to eternity
is usually only classified
    codified and recorded in history
    as under 'missed opportunities'.

What clues are there in the eye of the beholder
or the handshake of a friend of a friend
    on a blind date with your mask to decode as
"Oh, this is the big 'O' ?"

Opportunities are as scarce as angels
     but with better disguises
creative chameleons
whimsical bastards that tantalize us
     from the other side of the dance floor
we see their movements, a bit of a shape
     through their rhythmic limbs that separate us
in our eagerness, our desperate despairing
we clutch at any round symbol or cycle
believing that it is 'O'
     yes, our completion

our mouths struggling for that perfect oval
     as we lock in embraces
surely, this one, this time,
this 'O',
          o   OO   oo
                              O

JANUARY JAUNT

Those crows' four jarring notes
signalling all to separate corners
sliced sunlight and grey clouds
from black winter tree trunks
shook off remaining rusty leaves
from gun-metal stiff branches
slowed our tiring heart beats
as we swung gloved hands
unconnected.

MUCH LEFT ONE

Some claim they prefer leftovers
saying the flavour is richer
when warmed-up, even reheated
or that things are tastier
the second time around
though few buy the idea
that anyone really desires
the broken-in, well worn
comfortable, rough edges gone
trained and taught to follow
used but not used-up
discarded, rejected ones.

So, what about the fourth encounter
or sixth sampling
or twentieth time and turn
turning over and over
of this much tried and tested, even true dish?

There are not infinite ways one can dress
up the same old main course;
how many times can one add new ingredients
or different spices to vary the same old recipe?

Scorched bits begin to stick to the pan
welcoming baking smells go up fan's exhaust
a few dried crumbs roll under the table
so servings grow smaller
as sweet sauce stays on the platter
until what was labelled nourishing
no longer resembles
the original treat;

all remains go to landfill.

24

WANTING HIM DEAD

Maybe I can't yet
but still certain
that I could snuff him.
Now stuffing him in a sewer
I like that cuz it's drowning
in crap like he spews on me
too many Saturday nights

or tis already Sunday morning
cozy, clean sheet for me
leaving him *starkers*
on damp cement floor
no window, no breeze
let him freeze in his own mess
no more boozy, cigar breath
for me.

Each day he rules
on my sweat, on my dime
grinds into me
paring more of me
into dead scrapings
once hollowed
my shell will crumble
on its own, all dust.

Ok, maybe, push his prick
into a slow meat grinder;
Not yet ready with scissors
scythe nor sabre
fence post, snake pit nor poison

still, I dream, I scheme, I plan …

26

OUTING

Not every ex takes you
for an outing to an outhouse
also to admire his hand
built mountain retreat
his latest city escape.

On a perfect June day
as the truck rattled and grumbled
up the steep logging road
we're switch-backed into memory
    so much to unload
shit that should have been
    buried decades ago
such dry and flaky grudges
not even rich enough for manure
    grow to new connections.

Once we were at 'outs'
but now this outing frees us
    no more hidden agendas
we are separate and whole
    in our new lives

Our children now grown
to new paths and flyways
searching for their own outhouses
to unload their unneeded histories,
letting their futures be dungfree.

28

REUNION

Spare me these misnamed meetings
with ghosts from the past
forerunners of horrors to come –

How can you reunite those
who were never joined
in the first place?

Class reunion, family reunion
showing   how different & difficult
we all are,   as each plays
judge and recorder
scoring up profits and losses –
so many sighs and signs
of hair dyes, bifocals and implants

Each operation and tragedy   related
in enthusiastic   boring detail –
I've already heard too many tales
of ailing parents, dying children and
missing, and naturally unaccounted for, spouses

What a hoax, this attempt to party:
to make a cheerful noise together
as if the unshared twenty-five years
could be gulfed and erased
somehow a concentrated effort
at creating a mass memory
a shared something or other
from back when, could fool us
all into feeling young again

and even if we found our youth:
could we use it today?

OK, I always go,   hogging the limelight
as a clown.

BRAIN DIETING

BUBBLES IN THE THINK TANK

Exhausted, eating chocolate daily now
but my sugar highs fade faster each time
so much energy sapped
by trying to dam up, just silence
bad thoughts, evil images

racing with busy fingers
from club projects
to fancy gifts and gatherings
striving to cram my head with details:
clear glue here, red paint there
add frosting and blue candles
remember Jerry's joke

smiling, laughing, wanting a hug
in return
but always alone in the battle

bashing down impulses
beat for bruises, cause bleeding
in all those look-a-way faces
cross-the-road bodies
avoiding me, needy me:
air pockets bursting.

POPPYCOCK

Maybe it was pop's penis
that caused
what you label: my symptoms
but why should I give you
details for free?

You're getting paid for just
listening
who gives me big bucks
for recounting painful fucks?

34

WAITING ROOM

Sometimes there is no room
to wait, stand up straight
let white wall support spine
each disc and joint protesting
this latest exclusion.

Others slump in silence
or slouch on barely padded chairs
rustling pages of old magazines
flipping past ads, continuous ads
of what they can never own nor be:
all impossible dreams of *Reality TV*.

Skinny teen drums fingers,
Granny sniffles, dabbing eyes
Bacteria fighting soap doesn't
overpower sweat of fear
leaking from these distressed bodies
in this doctor's prolonged pause:

already have been sentenced.

SAFETY CATCH

Numb is also painless
shut down all small senses
snuggle knees to chest
in this charcoal capsule

from here you can't see
their judging eyes pretending
claiming to measure you

move in further, even lose
your tingling fingers and toes
soundless, weightless
float in this dark
no scent of others near
finally separated from fear

true aloneness, still hopeless:
that's the catch of safety.

LISTING

Clutching list on that cardboard
back to my cheques
should I have my diary, too?
Patting my pocket, yes, my pencil

My turn soon, only two ahead
don't look at her middle red eye
don't hear his hissing breath
as he floats overhead
no one else knows he's been
following you, since midnight

Tell doctor to make it go away
first request on my list
always worst at the top
get doctor, hear it
hovering 'specially in the dark
night light doesn't work
only TV on low, flashing
lets me sleep, keeps me safe.

BRAIN WAVES

Coated wires hooking
to clicking machines
blue and cream lights
flickering, pulsing
across numbered screens

Coated doctors looking
pencil flashlights probing
my dry eyeballs sting
scalp itchingly sore
smelly antiseptic salve

Being de-bugged outside and in
as current surges through bone
grey matter quivers out messages
squiggly red lines chart
themselves on graph paper
just another whispering machine

Ceiling mirrors repeat my monster head
electrodes spike my metallic cap
whatever your current theory
or whatever named fancy digits,
I ain't no Frankie teen, you idjits!

PIXILATED

Come, fairy queen
lead my stumbling steps
to flowered forests
Lethe-laced streams
bird and breeze symphonies
skin tingling pleasures

leaving impatient horns
and screeching brakes
of so-called traffic jams
just jam against me, fairy queen
dream dance me away

Come, wingèd angels
lift me on high
let your harps sigh
as smiles sail by

let clock scheduled duties
stay gravitated to earthly plots
dissolving yesterday's fears
to rainbowed galaxies.

CUSTOMARY STANDARD

A carpenter wants us all
at right angles
straight lines without deviations.

Norm is so mechanical
factory reproduction:
    every tire tread evenly
    set to flatten
artists into blandness
inventors into monotony.

Norm has no ribbons nor medals:
no bronze, silver nor gold
no excelling, nor failing
    no statues of David
    no Songs of Solomon
    no God-believing Einstein.

Standardized people = cookie cutter citizens
patterned for customary morés:
such mores make us less.

ADDICTIVE CREATING

RED APPLES

for John Brezinskis' Trio

Lush, rush, but never crush
vibrant red apples spill silently
from overflowing bowl
nestling on soft silk cloth
mirroring in crystal.

All inviting my empty hands
     my tongue.
I want to bite one of your apples
lick the paint from your fingers
taste the creativity of your eye.

Nearby, your reflecting lemons promise
more than "a host of golden daffodils"
and there is nothing ghostly
in your succulent, gleaming
red, yellow, green peppers
just all flavours to savour.

43

Your feast for eyes
serves a banquet of memories
of such richness: fruit and wine
shared piquant salads
and of more tactile games.

Your face gleaming in silver
repeated in crystal
– sour lemons of life ignored –
just you, a creator
inviting with vibrancy
enough for all.

44

FRAGMENT

Such are our lives:
bits and pieces of candlelight dinners
then melted wax colouring our memories
like mud stains on linen cloths
that refuse to fade
yet smears to the edges lighten
keeping us separate, distanced
by time and flow.

Rose buds offer us curved lines
as do shared sunset clouds
a softness to challenge our hard angles
that square of table cloth
those straight copper candle sticks
in eternal cycles
we are that unnatural fragment.

PRIMARY SOURCE

Driftwood: waves shaping or man carving
even a piece of a tree
is a part of growth:
a reaching to the sky
a kneading into the earth
light outer edge of grain
inner dark heart exposed
but strong and resounding with beats
flowing from smooth hollows
to inner crusty curves
unexpected openings
inviting us into its centre
never a straight ruler
always the unique
letting us be individuals
    and finding belief
in this sculpture –
from a primary source.

SELF-PORTRAIT

This artist's hand
that takes direction
from her head and heart
handling her visions
is giving us handles
in sizes and shapes.

Her black, mud-colour and grey smudges
share just three shapes
her thumb and two fingers
with rounded nails
her markers left smeared on canvas
just like a telltale tombstone
these are her self-stones.

Strong fingers imprinting
   imp printing her self-print
I.D. - id - indelible traces
art shaping our viewers' view:
her self-portrait creates our mirror.

THIS BIRD WITH A BULLET
IN ITS BILL

Red-breasted, white throated
lime-green feathered
this bird flies off
with the metal evidence.

Tough and tropical, the Jacamar
is said to eat buzzing
honey bees for appetizers.

This long white beak
like a bony gun barrel
crunches soft wasp bodies
in half, each mouth-sized
morsel swallowed whole.

Like magpies drawn by shine
perhaps the Jacamar
was intrigued by the blood
on the silver cylinder.

It's just a sidebar
mystery to what occurred
after the lethal shot
as birds usually tell all
not hide the music.

GOING FOR THE GOLD

Once in four years or annually,   always aware
that each record is eventually
surpassed, overtaken –

sports and science set their bench marks:
Olympic medals and Nobel prizes
that others use as their basis points
places to spring from, surge upward –

yet in the arts
world-class achievement glows forever:
a shine to spur others
to their own excellence
not to better or to bury others
but to achieve their own brightness

as individual artists
competing only with themselves
in redeeming humanity's individuality:
our unique creativity
golden.

TEDDY BEAR TED

Ted Plantos

Just envisage Ted now
sharing cigars and war stories
with Milton Acorn and Al Purdy
slurping frothy mugs
while they argue whose turn
it is to build their poet's cabin
Ted calming those two yelling hotheads
with his gentle, honest humour
  "If you want to hit something
    bang that hammer on some nails
      or we'll be stuck out here
      on this white cloud forever!"

50

BILL VACUUMS

bill bissett is cleaning up the world:
his lower case words supporting the 'lower' classes
as each capital is devoured by capitalists
who destroy crops while the homeless
scrape sidewalks for sustenance

his punctuation omissions are erasing pain
and shame,   his rhythms healing sorrow
as each period and comma are sucked back
as bland bankers demand more profits
from penniless pensioners

his voice with accepting laughter spells out
i've been there too /i'ph bean thair two!
so just cheer bissett onward
vacuuming into the void
those political injustices so powered by greed

leave bill singing in special form
random sounds chanting an elegy
for our fading wellness
for our lost wholeness.

MUSING ON SYLVIA PLATH
A 20th Century Poetic Comet

Why couldn't you wait, Sylvia?
Day dreaming, hoping to meet you
we were just young mothers
       struggling to find words
for the poems raging inside
       of us – summer of 1963 –
household dust, toddlers attached to knees
hungry husbands, demanding
       our creative energy
as our mouths opened
too often soundless
just small O's gaping
       dry tongued
       white teeth rimmed
our stilled caves of craving.

SAGGING

"Time is sagging,"   announces the emcee
dripping off Dali's painting
slipping through slats of the curved mike
smothered in 'dead air time'
from closed mouthed poets
lost in energy-less, muse-less smoke haze

for when time sags
we are all gagged,
just useless body bags
pointless, negative black holes
in a never-to-be universe

when infinity drips, eternity sleeps
then frozen motion gives up and dies
so our creativity ends
in silence
as one last loon
dives to the bottom
of the remaining blue lake.

SELF SLASHING

Reviewing, previewing
one's unwritten manuscripts
playing the hazardous game
of the objective critic
    mental censorship
constricting the seeding, the budding

what use are the great   one-liners
clunking out, unconnected
still-born thoughts
dead-end ideas, aborted
with bloody strain
pain in lifelessness
    the worry of hacking too much
off the mother bone
of eventually hitting crumbling
powdery white fossils

prejudging one's lines
before they feel the smack
of   keyboard letters black on white screen
      the lifeline cord cut only
when the published story kicks
off the page, yelling
"read me, pay attention" to the reader

endowed with enough energy
to keep breathing
through decades of being squeezed
between other volumes
on the library shelves
      all vying for the reader's
renewal stamp
and our immortality.

MASSAGING THE MEDIUM

Be subjective, be subject
merge with the music
speak for the spirit
of the thing not yet into word
flow with the flesh
creating the other

that which was always suspected
of hovering behind closed minds
just on the edge of dreamers
a shapeless force
a distorting presence
unnamed but insistent
pressuring for expectant success
against fear of emptiness
running dry

just a wisp-o'-the-willow
cutting the tender child's thoughts
so the missing leaf's shadow
scratches the (pre)memory
demanding (re)creation

fighting for form
begging to be shared
so tired of the void or
chaos of black holes
the seductiveness of absence
desiring light to mark edges
urging the definition of birth

only then (re)turning you both free
of that unknown burden
the heavy gloom of (pre)recognition
this waiting   for something to be.

SCRATCH

Scratching the scab of sadness
refusing to heal
wading chin deep and glorying
in our chosen victim self
picking pieces of skin off
to let a little blood seep
in public for pity
our whining overrides our reason.

Scabs are signs of healing:
a temporary mark, locating
the site of skin open to bone;
our bodies joining flesh to flesh
to seal our wounds, yet
our minds connecting horrors
not neutralizing those nightmares.

Invisible scars may remain
called painful, 'learning experiences'
as broken bones mend stronger than ever,
but not muddled, mis-fired minds
nor by-passed, brusied hearts.

BEYOND BELIEF

GLOVES

Foxgloves are never worn
by foxes nor fiends.
These pastel sentinels divide
green trees by their delicate bells
fully in charge of the wilderness.

Foxgloves need no promo agents
nor fancy sign posts;
their fans gaze adoringly
whether they are pink, white, mauve.

Each bell exquisite in itself
just as we are:
        all God's creations
unique gloves for our souls.

MYSTERY

Candle flame: cream and yellow
widest at its black wick
tapering and flickering
deeper orange at the tip
of its arrowhead
then unseen into almost blue air
it gives its greatest heat
blistering innocent fingers.

Light invisible to my eye
I am seared inside
by Your purifying flame:
a heat beyond ken or measure
leaving no smoke nor ash
just myself refined in Your fire
- a blazing tongue.

SOL

Our two-faced friend is
cancer searing
our blond northern sisters
while scorching crops
of southern brothers.

We raise our faces towards
your glowing hopeful dawns
we bow in praise
to your blazing sunsets
thankful for another
of your days.

O perpetual radiation
we cannot control you
O terrible necessity
with earth, air and water
for our bodies
Outliving us all, yet

not feeding our soul
you cannot control
our spirit.

WATER WORLD

Enter a wet world
where water caresses
your shoulders and thighs
– far away from trouble

let bubble bath foam
or herbal salts soothe
your aching limbs
or let your arms and legs
float in warm suds
– far away from trouble

or splash and sigh
in shower gel
rinse and terry towel
to tingling freshness
– far away from trouble

or slide into heated pools
or swim in sun-danced lakes
or stroke in moon-splashed seas
to be water supported
your burdens carried
– far away from trouble.

WALK BAREFOOT

Fling your flimsy sandals
    and steel-toed boots
over your left shoulder
    into the recycling bin
drop your sweaty runners
    and spike high heels
into closeted, old shoe boxes.

Let your heels know
supple sand and gritty gravel
let your arches mould
into lake bottom muck
and rich garden soil
let your toes pattern
the dusty crust of earth:
our terra firma.

This earth that grows your food
that shares its building
minerals, rocks and stones
that supports trees
for your oxygen
that creates landscapes
that teach you awe:
   their incredible variety
   never-ending mysterious beauty.

Feel your nurturing earth.

POWER MAD

Logic does not rule in chaos
there is no ruler to measure a trap
for unreason, nor poison or serum
against shapeless, senseless fear.

Take any fear
none is self-limiting
some sort of pulsating life
just sits coiled
awaiting the tired brain
to relax its reason.

Then fear springs in circles
of expanding glee
to colour all grey cells black
with its icy projections
of coming pain and despair.

Fear expands every crack
until sanity breaks
as rational barriers bounce.

Fear is power mad
never satisfied except
with the devoured ego.

PARASITIC

Doubt is the most addictive needle of all
pain that thrills the intellect
slivers our delight by pricking
each ballooning bubble of optimism

shards that shear so cleanly
through hypocrisy
that bloodless, lifeless tumour
seems a thing of humour
a half-forgotten rumour
no longer threatening
just a normal growth

Doubt can be our badge of honour
a medal of a martyr
the skeptic's stamp of approval
of damning criticism

Doubt, a jaundiced cynic's medicine,
an anti-acid for syrupy sentimentality

Doubt, symbiotic narcotic
a useful antidote for the hype and hyper-
bole of our super, duper, latest,
ad sale life style we race in

but fatal in overdose
Doubt castrates creativity.